Truffle Hound
Luke Kennard

VERVE
POETRY PRESS
BIRMINGHAM

PUBLISHED BY VERVE POETRY PRESS
Birmingham, West Midlands, UK
www.vervepoetrypress.com
mail@vervepoetrypress.com

All rights reserved
© 2018 Luke Kennard

The right of Luke Kennard to be identified as author if this work has been asserted in accordance with section 77 of the Copyright, Designs and Patents Act 1988.

No part of this work may be reproduced, stored or transmitted in any form or by any means, graphic, electronic, recorded or mechanical, without the prior written permission of the publisher.

FIRST PUBLISHED SEP 2018

Printed in Birmingham by Positive Print

ISBN: 978-1-912565-07-8

CONTENTS

Ibuprofen Song	4
A.I.	6
Some People Are Special But Then They Immediately Ruin It	7
Ghost Story	8
Filter	12
"'Nova Satus': Nova Satus (Nova Satus)"	18
Benediction	22
Parallel	23
Migraine	25
Review	28
Children's Party Meal	29
The Plagiarism Officer	30
If You Were Truly Awake It Would Be Unbearable	32
Accountability	33
Italicise This	35
Acknowledgments	

Ibruprofen Song

You can always find someone far more intelligent and someone way stupider than you so whether you're feeling really bad about yourself or, contrariwise, you're worried you might be getting conceited, it's very easy to recalibrate – you only have to wander around for a bit and talk to some people. It works with anything: virtuous/evil; beautiful/ugly; pedantic/permissive; disillusioned/idealistic.

Take me: I was writing a song about 39p ibuprofen – the kind you can get from a newsagents behind the counter. The song was set in a newsagent, a badly lit one and it was partly about how it's weird newsagents still exist, and partly about how cheap ibuprofen is, like maybe one of the cheapest substances on earth and they should build pink and white houses with it.

But then I started thinking about a music critic and the music critic wrote *Most people write songs about serious and momentous subject matters but Kennard can make poetry out of a packet of off-brand ibuprofen.* And I felt 1. that wasn't fair on most people and 2. it wasn't even true, really, and I felt so annoyed I wanted to scream. I thought momentarily of cramming so many ibuprofen into my mouth – there are always plenty of boxes in my house, only two pills missing, hungover newsagent mornings – and crunching through their sugar shells, washing it down with a cold cup of steeped, leftover coffee so that if it didn't kill me it would likely do permanent damage to my stomach; you can always find someone with a more permanently damaged stomach than you and, conversely, someone who has taken great care over their diet.

You can find someone who will say I love you, because you are a rucksack, and someone who will say I love you because you are a necklace made of unshelled nuts, a string threaded with brazil nuts, hazelnuts, almonds and walnuts you have drilled a hole in. The nuts inside the shells are, of course, desiccated, mummified, inedible. You cannot blow a nut like an egg, that is absolutely certain, so the only alternative, if you are to make a necklace of nuts, is to leave the nut inside.

But me, I love you because you are a necklace of pink ibuprofen tablets, the technical part of a sunset, statement heels, ironic lip-gloss, P45 pink, a tiny hole drilled in the middle with a very fine drill and then varnished and then a tinier hole drilled through the set varnish before they are threaded and attached to a clasp from an online jewellery supplier. We will always help one another fasten our ibuprofen necklaces, singing my ibuprofen song like mosquitoes before they mate, driven by frequency alone.

You can always find a month which is July and a month which is March. You can always find someone who seeks to find more significance in the month than you and someone who dismisses not just that, but other things as well, someone who doesn't believe in any of the things. And we can call them embattled ghosts frying in butter during a power cut, frying slowly, in butter, during a power cut, during the best power cut, during the great power cut between you and me and everything we wanted. You can always find someone who will say, there, just there, and stop your giant mosquito heart like a door.

AI

It is very easy to create an AI indistinguishable from a human being because all any of us really cares about is how we come across. The algorithm required to replicate this is embarrassingly simple, more Magic 8 Ball than Deep Blue. Me, for example: all I ever do is agree with people and hope that they'll leave me alone. An AI version of me would be a nodding dog on the parcel shelf of a 1980s hatchback. You are better than me, but the AI version of you would just be the same nodding dog with a small tape recorder attached playing a loop of *Really? Is that really what happened? Is that really what you think?* And people would say, they are made for each other because they are so different. Nodding Dog 1 is sweet but subservient, while Nodding Dog 2 doesn't suffer fools gladly and somehow it works because opposites attract. Do you, nodding dog, take this other nodding dog, forsaking all others... *Yes. Really? Is that really what happened? Yes.*

Some People Are Special But Then They Immediately Ruin It

They seem to hear music in a way many of us can't. They listen to Radio 3 on a crappy little shower radio in the shape of a seahorse, its speaker holes half gummed up with something from when the radio was used for its intended purpose, suckered onto a bathroom tile, and not their only means of listening to music. Now they have fallen on hard times and it is their only means of listening to music. Yet they appear to enter a state of spiritual bliss as they listen, moving around the room in a trance, the seahorse radio propped against a stack of saucepans from which the Teflon coating is starting to bubble and flake off like dyshidrotic dermatitis. They move around as if in a trance, plucking things out of the air. What? wisps of cotton? tiny switch cords? It's quite annoying. We ought to cherish their ability to transcend their reduced circumstances via an art form about which we are, at most, dilettantish. At the very least we ought to allow it without passing comment – but we find ourselves resenting them. Resenting them more than the audiophile bore with his golden speaker cables and £8,000 separates system who we might accuse, more than anyone, of missing the point.

Ghost Story

This is a ghost story about a 9 year old boy who is so afraid of ghost stories he has to go to great lengths to avoid hearing them. We say "ghost stories", but there are rarely any ghosts in our ghost stories. There are serial killers, perhaps some strange and unexplained things on the periphery, the suspicion of an uncanny nightmare, but our ghost stories usually just amount to elaborately creative suffering. Weird that we conflate the two genres, as if our innate cruelty is somehow supernatural. Or maybe it isn't. Weird, I mean. I don't know. That the serial killer is not a British phenomenon is more geographical than socio-political. Imagine a vast Britain, the size of Russia. We'd have hundreds of thousands of serial killers. Home Counties serial killers, once the heat was on, would flee thousands of miles to the State of Yorkshire.

Anyway, the 9 year old boy, if he hears one, a ghost story, through inattention to his surroundings (camp fire, school trip youth hostel dorm, picnic bench in a cold, grey lunchtime), or say his curiosity gets the better of him, or say he wants to see if he's toughened up since last time, desensitised, become less of a fucking pussy... If he hears a good ghost story, he spends weeks afterwards experiencing symptoms more usually associated with PTSD. Insomnia, night terrors, distraction, loss of appetite and ability to think about anything else. This is from hearing one ghost story. He turns it over and over in his head like a beloved or problematic memory, examining it from every angle, filling in the backstories and embellishing the dialogue. A three minute tale in the oral tradition becomes a saga, a tetralogy, in the ensuing weeks. He cannot tell his parents what's eating him because passing the story on seems somehow shameful, as if the story itself is cursed and he cannot imagine the story not having the same effect on anyone else as it has had on him. This is also in-keeping: the hexed tape, the occult book, the blighted photograph; the act of telling and retelling a form of haunting.

He realises, at this point in his life, that he cannot really imagine anyone else's mind. What would it be like to have a mind which doesn't react to ghost stories like a slug to salt? His contemporaries, for instance, seem to be capable of telling the most sadistic and harrowing story of atavistic/nihilistic dread, rage, madness, torture, bereavement as if it were a dirty joke. Moments later they are projecting the shadows of their semi-erect penises onto the youth hostel dorm walls with their torches.

Is the issue that, in listening to the stories, he always identifies with the victim? Like Berryman with newspapers – "including the corpses, pal" (Dream Song 53, p.60). That the tormented family is always his own? That he is the mother and the tortured child? Didn't Haneke say something, on Funny Games, that if you don't want to watch this film, you don't need to. Is the trick to imagine it's someone else's family? Someone you don't give a shit about? He's not making any case for his superior humanity here, but how are you supposed to care that little? Genuine question. I mean he doesn't think this now, because adulthood is maybe characterised by not giving a shit. But at the time it was a genuine question. He puts his hand under his bed so that his dog can lick it – something he often does for comfort – but whatever licks his hand... it feels more like a person's tongue than a dog's. He retracts his arm and lies perfectly still.

The next night he gets into bed with his parents. He is 11, not 9, I was lying. He cries. He tries to explain the story, but he edits out so many of the unpleasant bits – to spare them – that the twist doesn't really make any narrative sense. His father wants to have a word with other children's parents to ask them to stop telling inappropriate stories. *Oh my god, please don't.* Still, they are very patient, at 3am, maybe a little dismayed that their 11 year old son can't cope with hearing a ghost story, but they love him. His mother strokes his hair until he falls asleep.

The next night his father says, 'Okay, let's take a drive.' They are going on a drive to prove that there is nothing to be scared of. They park in a lay-by next to the forest. 'You wait here. I need to stand on top of the car to get phone signal,' says his father. 'I'll keep tapping the roof of the car with my foot so you know I'm safe.' But after some time the tap stops and is replaced by something which sounds more like a severed head being thunked against the roof of the car. The boy realises that he has left his mother alone in the house with whatever or whoever licked his hand the previous night. *I don't know why you're crying; I have to walk back out of this place by myself.*

He undoes his belt and assumes the foetal position on the back seat of the car. When he was younger he was so scared of fire that he didn't like things which were orange. If all of his family were in the same room he'd sporadically go and check the other rooms of the house to make sure they weren't on fire. The rooms. There was an orange blanket which terrified him because it was the same colour as fire. His second-hand bicycle was orange and his father had to spray-paint it gold. He is certainly a very scared boy, we may say that much for him.

There is rumoured to be one ghost story which will literally scare him to death. It is cold and he is shaking and he is lying on the backseat of the car with his eyes closed very tight. He hears the window next to his head begin very slowly to open and he shuts his eyes tighter as if bracing for a blow. And then a soft voice, a gentle voice, begins to tell him the story. *A family lived in a Victorian terraced house in the East Midlands of the United Kingdom...*

This is the terrible price of being involved in mankind, the boy supposes. When you die you will live through every single human life ever lived, the billions. You will be murdered and you will murder. And far worse, of course, but we needn't dwell on that. You will make some pretty self-serving decisions about governance several times. And you will lose count of the millions upon millions of times you starve to death. You will be the victim and the perpetrator of every single act ever committed. And then God will say, 'Hey, you.' And the trick is if you remember who you were.

When the boy opens his eyes it is morning and he is sitting in the front seat of the car and he is 37 years old. His fingernails feel too long. The sky is page white. He turns the key in the ignition and the car won't start. It won't start. He tries again. It won't start. It won't start.

Filter

A filter is a material or fine, physical barrier, with minuscule holes designed to separate solid particles from a liquid or gas which passes through. To remove contaminants, impurities. A device which allows signals with certain properties to pass while blocking others. A measure of traffic control. The brain has the ability to filter information it considers non-essential.

I gave up smoking when my eldest son was born. This is embarrassing to admit as it amounts to something of a living platitude, a 21st century tradition, the new equivalent of Christening. *It is customary for the father to give up smoking.* An admission that he now has a reason to stay alive for as long as possible – whether or not the foundational damage has already been done: lung cancer; chronic obstructive pulmonary disease; heart disease; stroke; asthma; diabetes; blindness; cataracts; age-related macular degeneration; colon, liver, stomach and pancreatic cancer. The utter misery of not being able to breathe properly for years and then dying in excruciating pain. The filter of your lungs and bronchioles gummed up and useless. The price of a habit you didn't even enjoy very much.

When we were sixteen my friends and I smoked roll-ups without filters, picking bits of tobacco – *baccy* – from our lips and teeth as we smoked them. *Rollies.* I hate the English habit of assigning cute diminutives to everything. Rollies, uni, hollybobs Nation of idiots.

Our brands were Golden Virginia or Cutter's Choice. I preferred the latter: the oily, damp, finer-cut leaf which you extracted from the pouch in clumps like matted fur. The comparatively dry, bark-like Golden Virginia seemed to me less fresh and less enticing. I realise this was probably marketing, a chemical added to the product to make it seem juicy and freshly picked. Or it was just more tar; *now with added tar.* There was a cheaper brand called Drum which was drier still and tasted of creosote. I remember a soldier with a moustache on the packet. This was before cigarette packaging was out-lawed. We called normal cigarettes *straights* and hated them.

I wonder if the Before and After shots of a cigarette filter – white as a summer cloud to shitty, bumble-bee brown; pure to sullied – are also a form of marketing. If filters are designed to change colour via an unconnected chemical reaction, an additional chemical which is itself toxic, in order to exaggerate the colour change. Look at everything I've not taken into my body.

The body as filter.

The Hungarian inventor Boris Aivaz patented the first cigarette filters in 1925. He used crepe paper. The first filter-tipped cigarette to be marketed to a smoking public was the Viceroy from B&W in 1936. The filter was made of cork. I have whittled a cigarette filter out of a wine-bottle cork – it's not very nice, but the reason most contemporary cigarette filters are brown and illustrated with paler flecks is a visual reference to this; an imitation cork-tip. The cellulose acetate filter was patented in 1952, but it was two years later that the "Winston" achieved any kind of significant market penetration. How much else, I wonder, do I fail to decode? A picture of a cork on the end of a cigarette, a surname defining an ancestor's job, character, situation. The mere symbols we live with. This is not the world.

Later, at "uni" I smoked only after writing five hundred words of an essay. But this became two-hundred and fifty, then one hundred until, by reading week, I felt myself incapable of writing a sentence unless I had a lit cigarette in my hand. This was the early days of dial-up internet and people were still getting their heads around it. Spending upwards of an hour downloading a grainy three-minute pornographic film. People cutting off their own fingers. Snuff movies. A thirty-second film, I was told, of a woman saying *snuff movies do not exist* then being shot in the head. Some horrible curiosity bid me to stay in the room but some other force made me walk out and ignore my hall-mates laughing at me, before the clip had started. I was being a prude. I said I had some work to finish. When they told me about it later, over dinner, they were sad. One of them vowed to turn private investigator and find out who had made the film. There are things you take in which you can't put out again.

Inhale. From the Latin *inhalare*. Breathe in. Some things stay.

Cellulose acetate is a form of plastic which can take anywhere from 18 months to a decade to decompose. The last time I was in Paris I was given a €60 fine for flicking away my cigarette butt, which now makes more sense.

\-\-\-\-\-\-

Filtration is the process by which the particulate and gaseous phase of tobacco inhalation is modified. The smoke passes through the filter which removes the tar. The filter does nothing to remove several other toxins such as carbon monoxide. "Tar" is a resinous combusted particulate matter, an umbrella term for countless carcinogenic and mutagenic agents. All that has really changed is the type of tumour rather than the frequency.

\-\-\-\-\-\-

We sat under the vast canopy of a plum tree in my friend's garden. The plums grew high and dropped only once they were rotten, food for wasps and birds rather than humans. We revised for our Biology GCSEs. Chlorophyll, mitochondria, partially-permeable membrane.

\-\-\-\-\-\-

Boris Aivaz stood waiting for the ferry, his face absorbing the sea-flecked breeze. In his pocket an unopened letter from his wife. In his other pocket a silver cigarette case. Since cigarette packaging has been replaced with graphic images of the consequences, cigarette cases have become popular again. I once went to a Halloween party dressed as a health warning from a pouch of tobacco, with a false beard and a clear plastic sandwich bag of five hundred grams of minced beef strapped under my chin. The costume was initially amusing but the minced beef soon started to smell, and to spill, and I took it off, offering to make a chilli, which was refused.

My friend sees her faith as a kind of filter. To go through the filter of prayer, of Confession, repentance and communion is to be purged of all your vileness. To emerge, however temporarily, in a state of grace. To be fitted with a new filter. But to live is to use your filter. You are sullied again within a fraction of a second, a fraction of a thought. This is magical thinking. Or perhaps not. I am so in love with her I fantasise about being hit by a car when I cross the road. In my fantasy I am badly hurt but not so bad that I cannot text her, from the ambulance, *I have just been hit by a car.*

I would like to offer those I have hurt, those I have damaged, a better self. A filtered self. But this is only vanity. I mean I would like them to forget and still look well on me. To exhale it all. I would like everything I have done wrong to be non-essential information. The pulp and silt in a paper coffee strainer. The way it hits the bin with a wet thud.

To be filtered. To pass through a filter. To move from one world to the next. I have the book you left me. I finished it last night. We're experimenting with separate rooms so I have plenty of reading time. In his final entry Dosithy takes the decision to follow the demons behind the tree into an alternate world where he didn't become a hermit and served as a lowly Rassophore, tending to visitors, dusting the iconostasis. Before spending three years infirm and bedbound, cared for by juniors. Dying in confusion, his scowl tightening into an X. Is that enough? For now we see through a glass, darkly. Then face to face.

Where are you?

"'Nova Satus': Nova Satus (Nova Satus)"

So you have a sky and some fairly florid description of the sky and what's important is that it isn't *our* sky. There's an orange planet rising, roughly twice the size of our moon, and there are also three little moons which describe an arc to the right of the orange planet. Anastasia is standing at the long window of her simple condominium with her six year old daughter, watching the sky. She runs her hand through her six year old daughter's hair. Or maybe that's wrong; maybe that's the sort of thing you like to *think* you'd do under a new sky. Maybe Anastasia is watching the sky in fascination, as she has done for the last 434 nights, but her daughter is sitting at the table in the open-plan kitchen-dining area, playing a Match Four game on a very thin tablet and squealing in frustration. It's a Match Four game where you move and match planets in horizontal or vertical lines – no diagonals – and Anastasia's daughter is on level 36, and far in excess of her screen-time-limit which Anastasia has lost the heart to enforce, and maybe that's all *you're* doing right now in trying to describe the scene. Do you have to choose between *space kids are miraculous and we are so grateful* and *space kids can be a real pain in the ass*? Which combination will make the four planets disappear?

One of the three moons, the middle one – let's say they're the size of pool balls if our moon's a beach ball – is irregular, like a nugget. Anastasia's daughter calls this The Stupid Moon. The Stupid Moon is a different shape depending on its rotation. Sometimes it looks like a melting parrot, sometimes it looks like someone's head in a Francis Bacon painting, sometimes it looks like a big toe. And it's shiny, as if it might be a giant lump of gold.

At some point you're going to have to describe the other two moons even if there isn't very much to say about them. Likewise bureaucracy, the perfect and imperfect systems, the selfless public servants and venal self-publicists – this is, let us remember, not our public. Likewise agriculture and diet. Mushrooms are easy to cultivate. Leathery dark green leaves which are tough but very good for you. And a meat substitute which grows on slides from a single cell and, with the right sauce, is all but indistinguishable from the real thing. Anastasia, actually, is now celebrated on Earth for the very scandal she fled which, at the time, not only ruined her reputation but gave her legitimate fear for her own (and her family's) safety. Just change it. Don't tell anyone. Make all the fast-food chains secretly vegan and just don't tell the fuckers. See if they even notice. That was after the second Great Beef War of 2___. At some point you are going to have to write a tedious prequel. The Cow's Crusade. Maybe it can be outsourced.

At this point Anastasia wanders over to her daughter (you can say that she "abandons her twilight vigil" or something like that) and actually does run her hand through her hair, but her daughter says 'Mum,' with two syllables and shakes her head violently. The family set-up should emerge naturally within the first couple of pages. Maybe her husband went with them but his "heart was never really in it" and he resented Anastasia, perhaps he'd secretly harboured these resentments for a long time, of her success and relative profile, (let's say in spite of this being the 2_th century he's still secretly victim to the idea that as the "man" he should essentially be the provider with all the power that entails and felt jealous that his own work was comparatively, et cetera) but now that she had literally forced them into interplanetary exile he was no longer able to contain them, the resentments, and the relationship didn't last long in the colony and they're both with new partners now. Or maybe, in the colony, people are fairly relaxed about sex. Maybe we've taken the opportunity of a fresh, post-Enlightenment start to do away with notions of attachment and ownership and with them sexual exclusivity, so that you might meet a friend for a coffee and you might also have sex with them. You're going to have to consider whether this take on sexuality tends to foreground the masculine. Isn't it a utopian trope because the golden age of science fiction was largely written by bed-ridden war-vet horn-dogs too tired or unwell to masturbate? Maybe that doesn't matter. Maybe the truly compassionate thing is to gently but forcefully jerk them off. What now?

Maybe, that being the case, Anastasia's ex is still on the scene and they actually have a pretty good relationship and that'll be him now. You would like the doors to be automatic and very quiet but actually energy needs to be conserved and the doors are just doors. Light wooden doors because the climate is tropical and – this is going to need some unpacking – there's no crime. This is problematic because any organised system is really a form of crime and there can be no bureaucracy without criminality and vice versa; this is, anyway, how Anastasia feels. Maybe this story will turn out to be about the first murder. You're getting that dull feeling in the pit of your stomach again. What are you really trying to say about human nature? That's very important. Anyway, Kevin is here and Anastasia's daughter immediately drops her tablet and goes to him and he says something sitcomy like 'Hi, pumpkin!' and runs his hands through her hair and Anastasia feels a pang of-- The conflict you're creating is boring. This is no better than the first murder. They eat a thick mushroom stew and then they play a board game about terraforming which involves a surprising amount of character-creation and world-building for what is, essentially, a worker-placement mechanic.

Here's the thing: there is some concern – it is the subject of many op-ed pieces – that some of the new émigrés are in fact former beef gangsters. I mean of course they are. The chancellor himself was a general on the wrong side of the conflict, but he fully repented. This new wave is different, though. Oh, they've suffered and have visible and invisible scars to prove it, that's certain. But how would we know if they didn't have some ulterior motive for coming here? This is why Anastasia takes a sedative before reading her daughter a story about a robot who can't stop crying. So that she falls asleep at the same time, one arm under her daughter's neck, The Stupid Moon imperceptibly turning, turning, so that it resembles a badly damaged human ear. This is... I don't know. I'm not sure if this is going anywhere. This is why Kevin sits up in his buggy all night outside the condo, watching the glittery, plastic road. The roads are made of recycled vinyl records. Drive slowly and you can hear *bury my body lord I don't care where they...* That's rubbish. Scrap it.

The first little moon is. The third little moon is. The orange planet, which is now setting and half-visible on the horizon, appears large enough that you can make out craters in high-definition, chemical seas, an inexplicably long and straight crevasse which cambers a little, but only a little, almost like a smirk.

Benediction

I remember Kirk, a taller, muscular boy with brown hair, always ski-trip tanned, pushing our heads, and the gesture was not supposed to be kind; it was, in fact, meant only to be dismissive, slightly violent / menacing even, in part literally to stop us following the other boys around the back of the French building where they were talking (other boys who we didn't especially admire but desperately wanted/needed to be accepted by, although they disliked us and found something about us embarrassing, annoying, still decidedly child-like at the age of 14 which, in their defence, we were), so, yes, a minor act of bullying / exclusion, poor Rudolph, which was not supposed to be kind but in its very physicality – Kirk's hands pressed into our neatly centre-parted haircuts (which flicked out, moustache like at the edges, despite various mousses and waxes we had started asking our parents to buy for us as we were really trying to fit in), both of his palms pressed against our heads like melons or bowling balls, pushing hard so that we both instinctively started running on the spot, little tethered bulls, charging uselessly – which made us, the three of us, including Kirk, start laughing in a moment of (I hope this doesn't sound excessive) communion and shared humanity in acknowledgement, tacit on Kirk's part, gratefully, thirstily received on ours, that the conditions of our lives in this context we took so seriously and the social capital we markedly, conspicuously lacked was essentially arbitrary, which made me realise that touch, that being touched, in and of itself is et cetera et cetera et cetera

Parallel

A forty-one year old man returns to his family home for Christmas and immediately regresses. *Don't want that cup. Want Spiderman.* A straw articulated into the side as part of its web pattern. A crouched image of Spiderman, solemn as a pallbearer, mouthless face damaged in the dishwasher, hairline crack in the straw. *It's ruined. As you well know*, says his father. The man kicks the sideboard, which comes away from the wall. They distract him with *A Muppet Christmas Carol* and a family-size box of Frosties, which he eats by the handful. He winches the piano stool as high as it will go, kicks his legs. *Weeeeeeeeeee!* he says. *Stop looking at me*, says his sister, an intellectual property lawyer taking one of her three days off a year. The way she finds herself talking to him... it makes her eyes feel heavy and oversized. He is chewing her iPhone. *Stop chewing my iPhone!* His brain is fitfully illuminated: the blinking fairy lights' silent anthem. Thank you for the tree lights. He prays this. Thank you. The ends of cigarettes put out by a single drop of fat rain. Thank you for the parallel circuit, so that if one light goes out we know which to change, and thank you for the series circuit, so that if one light goes out we are all ruined. Is his family a parallel or a series circuit? He begins to cry. By Christmas day he is reduced to the mental state of a baby. He cries for three hours then has a nap next to the dog for fourteen minutes. When he wakes up he cries for four hours. The mother strokes his head. *Help me*, says the father. *Help me hold him*. She takes his legs. The father takes his shoulders. *What shall we do with the drunken sailor?* they sing. He cries harder. They rock him like a slow battering ram. His sister finds his favourite tree decoration, a silver bell. They hang it from a low branch and nudge it with his head until the ringing sends him to sleep. They turn on the radio:

a Christmas service. Crackly woman's voice reads the words of Simeon, *a sword shall pierce your own heart also*. And slowly, thinks the father. The man sleeps. The father knocks back a gin and tonic from the Spiderman cup. No ice. He makes a face. The mother reads a *Tragic Lives* digest, abridging eight of the year's best abuse memoirs into one tidy volume, bible-sized. She has not switched on the Kindle her daughter bought her. *You can make the font bigger*, she sighs. *I thought it would be useful*. The father snaps a cork in a bottle of pre-mulled wine. He pokes it into the bottle, muttering. *Look*, says the sister, *look, he's laughing*. And it's true, in his sleep, his mouth a bow, the man is silently convulsing as if party to some private joke with God. They stand around him and watch. He looks so happy. *Shhh*, says the mother. The phone rings. The man opens one eye, a look of alarm. *Hush now*, they say to him, together. He opens the other eye. His lower lip trembles. *Hush now*, says his sister, alone this time.

Migraine

For some time I had seen an autocue which told me what I should and shouldn't do and say. The autocue would run as a single line of white text, almost imperceptible, a little in front of my eyes. The words were legible, but faint enough that I could believe I was imagining it and, on the other hand, that it was entirely real. *Kick that can*, the autocue might read as I passed an empty can of Coca Cola lying in the gutter. And I would kick it. *Kick it again*. I would do so and, thus placated, the autocue would allow me to get on with my day.

When I met my future partner in line at the post office, the autocue read: *Talk to her*. And I did. A year later everything was going well, but she suffered from a terrible migraine which could leave her bed-ridden in a darkened room for days on end. The autocue said, *Share the migraine*.

So it was settled: we'd share the migraine. At first I wanted to take the migraine four days a week, but she told me not to make any grand gestures. 'If you do that, you'll end up using it against me,' she said. 'You won't want to, but you will. We'll just do 12 hour shifts.'

There are certain things... I had... I had suffered from this for some time. A sense, when I spoke, that I wasn't getting it across, what was in my head. And an increasing sense that what is in my head is quite urgent. And I mean "quite" as in completely. Quite urgent and impossible to express. I don't need to tell you this. We all get that. It's probably all we ever really communicate to one another. When I feel loved it's when I see that in someone else's eyes:

I know – it's terrible, isn't it? That's when I want to hug them. *I love you. Thank you.* And that's how it was with her. This is what drew me to her, as much as the autocue.

Parties were different: 'I'll take the migraine tonight,' she'd say, even if it wasn't her turn. 'You enjoy yourself.' And the pain would siphon out of my head and into hers. If one of us went away on business, the other would take the migraine for a full weekend.

I'm not saying we never argued. Sometimes I'd say to her, *You're killing me with your fucking migraine – I want to rip my own face off.* And she'd say, *How do you think I feel when you say things like that to me when it was your idea to share the migraine in the first place?*

One morning I refused to take the migraine ever again. She was horrified and, actually, I was horrified too. It was as if the autocue I had been reading for the last five years had been taken over by a less good person. I sat there wanting to laugh about it. 'You *knew* what you were getting yourself into,' she said. 'I told you not to get involved with me if you couldn't cope with the migraine. Furthermore, *I never asked you to share it.*'

'I'm not going to take the migraine any more,' I said, 'I'm just not.' There were tears in my eyes. She said I was just like every other man she'd ever been with – that they'd all done the *exact* same thing. Personally, I like to think I stuck it out a little longer.

Two days later I woke up with my own migraine. I took some letters down to the post-office for weighing, the migraine sloshing around in my head like bleach. She was standing in the queue.

'You look awful,' she said. 'Are you,' I said, trying to concentrate through the dancing white strings in my peripheral vision, 'are you doing anything tonight?' 'No,' she said. The autocue said that I should take her in my arms. 'But I don't really want to see you.' The autocue said that I should remonstrate and beg for forgiveness. 'Okay,' I said. 'I'm sorry, for what it's worth.' 'I know,' she said, 'thank you.' The autocue said that I should pursue her.

I turned to the counter and pointlessly shuffled the envelopes in my hands.

Review

I take a dating columnist to a pop-up restaurant in the silk district. We sit with our legs in the water of a deep and narrow pool. We each have little silver fishing rods instead of cutlery, a new testament wood-fire in a skillet between us. Presently I feel the line jank like a bad thought and reel in a horrified, pulsating squid. The dating columnist catches nothing. I put the squid on my hand like a glove puppet. I make it say to her: *These are the terrible excuses that men make for taking anything they want.* The fire isn't hot enough to cook the squid. We eat it raw. 'This is the worst idea for a restaurant,' I tell her. 'You forget,' she says, 'it's not the restaurant that I'm reviewing.'

Children's Party Meal

I am alone in the house. Seeing a pineapple squatting in the corner of the kitchen gives me the idea: I will prepare myself a children's party meal. I scalp the pineapple, cut off its bark and dice the flesh. I take a block of Extra Mature Cheddar and cut it into cubes and then I skewer one piece of pineapple and one piece of cheese onto 57 cocktail sticks. Some of them I go with cheese first then pineapple, some of them pineapple first then cheese because it is important to cater to both preferences. I arrange them on a large plate, the points of the cocktail sticks upward. Then I open every bag in a multipack of crisps and I mix them, Salt and Vinegar, Cheese and Onion, Smokey Bacon and Ready Salted, together in a large bowl. I open two packets of party rings and arrange them in a single layer on a tray. The neon and pastel shades of their icing. I take a large bag of Wotsits and a large bag of Hula Hoops and I insert the Wotsits into the Hula Hoops one by one. I use up a loaf of bread making cheese, ham and jam sandwiches which I chop into triangles and cut off the crusts. I have two 2.5 litre bottles of Fanta and a paper cup with stars on it. I arrange everything on the dining room table. I take a roll of POLICE LINE DO NOT CROSS tape which shouldn't really be in my possession and I wrap it around every chair until the table is cordoned off. I set up an easel and a low table with a pallet and some acrylic paints and I begin working on a photorealistic still life; the natural light is bad, and this is good. Perhaps you will say that I am wasting time and resources, or even that I am misdirecting that one talent bestowed on me, but what does it matter when I am alive and know myself to be alive perhaps most of all when my decisions are arbitrary and inexplicable? And, really, by this point, what choice do I have?

The Plagiarism Officer

Perhaps you will come up with three fake poetry collections: *The Sky Before It Rains* (2001); *God's Money* (2004); *Withering* (2013). Or perhaps you will be drawn back to speculative fiction, the way a dog is drawn. Try this. The day Anna B. finished her training she had a bad cold. She tried to hold her head still in the crowded lecture theatre and sniff as quietly and efficiently as possible. Dr Blend, a tall, thin man whose bald head accentuated his worry lines, was coming to the end of his 8th and final orientation talk. 'Over the term we have demonstrated,' he said, 'that education is the frontline. My final job is to tell you that the three case-studies you wrote your assignments on – including the struggling student of the fake teacher who had undertaken his teacher training with a tutor who had forged his assignments under the aegis of a professor who, himself, a decade earlier, had obtained his 86,000 word doctoral thesis from an essay mill for a fraction of his tuition fees – were all made up. Including the links to newspaper articles and government policy. I created them for the purpose of the exercise. It was fairly straightforward. One of them I outsourced. There'll be time for questions afterwards.' Several hands had gone up. 'To cut corners,' said Dr Blend, worrying the ribbon of his lanyard, 'is perhaps the single, defining factor of our humanity. Our equivalent of camouflage.' He clicked to a slide of a brown owl, its eyes closed, perching in a desiccated tree – it was difficult, at first, to even discern the creature among the dried pulp it might have been carved out of. He clicked again and the owl-shaped growth opened its bright orange eyes, then took flight. 'It is too late to reverse or prevent any of this – many of you were born after the Burnley Water Scandal, but you'll be aware that the unit which finally exposed the malpractice and cover up were effectively an illegal NGO whose real motivations were personal gain, and some of whose operatives were indirectly responsible for the initial violation of standards. Key figures on both sides are now in prison. But Burnley has potable water again.' He clicked to a slide of a glass of iced water. Anna was certain that the lights had dimmed a little, but it could have been an electrical fault or an hallucinatory effect of her fever. She remembered also that the man sitting next to her smelled of tinned tuna fish. 'I want you to understand that your job titles themselves are anachronisms,' said Dr Blend. 'We no longer stop plagiarism; we find the homeopathic solutions. Eventually you will accept that the resourcefulness your students show in working around your failsafe preventative measures, the ingenuity and creativity of the cheat, is what we are really testing them on. These are the transferable skills which will help them to thrive in the world. We are to live and work in the full knowledge – sorry,' he stopped to clear his throat, 'that we are the sample photographs that came with the frame.' And then he flickered and disappeared.

If You Were Truly Awake It Would Be Unbearable

We are not prepared and everything denies our chance; we have a feeling we are going to have to learn to play bridge one day and learn to like it, as if time could be canned. We don't process through streets, a plaintive trumpet, a body swaddled in white cloth. There is no last kiss. In England 9 out of 10 are slid inconspicuously into a furnace. I remember your face as if it were a logo. I do not remember what it represented. That everything is a form of love, a form of prayer, even data-entry, even processing purchase ledger invoices, is hard to bear in mind – a long commute. It occurred to me I miss you like a cat weighing up its chances at making a jump then thinking better of it, slinking away from the ledge. That I miss you more than the teacher's reference to Aristotle which flies over the heads of her students and I am the students. That there are no words in my language for how much I miss you so I have set off to travel to each country learning new words for how much I miss you and I have been doing this for two years now and in fact this is the sole reason we are apart.

Accountability

Unfortunately when I come round from the anaesthetic everyone is Luke Kennard and they have re-elected Luke Kennard. I cannot believe they've granted Luke Kennard a second term with an overwhelming majority after the damage he has already done. 'The *dogs*,' I say to my wife, Luke Kennard, who looks up from reading Martin Buber's *I and Thou*, a particularly sensitive birthday gift from our mutual friend Luke Kennard the previous year. At the job centre Luke Kennard is the usual bureaucratic prig when I tell him that I have been offered a job at Ladbrokes, but haven't taken it for personal reasons. 'It's where Luke Kennard wastes all of his money,' I tell him. 'It's where Luke Kennard pops out back to smoke three Pall Malls in a row then puts an ill-advised tenner on Luke Kennard in the 12:50 at Chantilly. And his partner, Luke Kennard, will want to know where the money is for nappies for their baby, Luke Kennard. I don't want to be a part of that.' Luke Kennard looks at me wearily, but he is trying to disguise that weariness with a "concerned frown" as if he has the first fucking idea about me and my life and my values. Next door in a subfusc room of the council offices which Luke Kennard has done an absolutely wretched job of cleaning at 6am this morning, Luke Kennard undergoes welfare assessment. 'And can I ask you,' Luke Kennard asks him, in his special "nice guy" voice, head tilted slightly to the left, his right, 'if it isn't too invasive a question, that is, if you tied your own shoes this morning? Luke Kennard huffs like a teenager. Luke Kennard is a murderous, patronising son of a bitch. 'Why?' sneers Luke Kennard. 'Can you get me a job in a shoe-tying factory?' Unfortunately he can, and Luke Kennard is soon tying the laces of nine hundred pairs of Converse All Stars a day, in spite of the fact that he is also dying of emphysema. *I gradually realised that writing opinion pieces had permanently damaged the way I write,* writes Luke Kennard in an op-ed piece with over six hundred shares. It is currently being read by Luke Kennard on his lunch break before he goes back to processing purchase ledger invoices for his boss, Luke Kennard, an essentially absent figure who just expects him to get on with things. Several thousand feet above this, Luke Kennard is off for a jolly to Barcelona just because. I get a Big Mac meal for lunch and Luke Kennard serves me in his little hat, his three gold stars for long service and yes I do want to go large, thanks Luke Kennard. Oh, yeah, Coke, sorry. I always forget to specify the drink and Luke Kennard has to ask me by saying *Drink?* in a voice which barely conceals his disdain. Luke Kennard hasn't bothered to bus his tray, so I do it for him as it's the only free seat; place is crawling with Luke Kennard. Luke Kennard is fairly unhappy today – an atmosphere of nebulous melancholy pervades the packed McDonalds – even though some of them must have voted for Luke Kennard themselves. I mean no, I wouldn't even dream of it: Luke Kennard is completely cut off from the experience of 96% of Luke Kennard, so voting for him and his Luke Kennards would be an act of self-destruction. But the alternative, Luke Kennard, wasn't exactly up to much either. It's easy to blame the Luke Kennard media, but really what were they to do when Luke Kennard just came across as desperate to be liked, as if he held himself to no other standard: a claw machine where everyone wins every time, but the prize is just a tiny sachet of popping candy and if you put your ear to Luke Kennard's mouth it's like you can hear the last rains of the Anthropocene extinction.

Italicize This

This is a story about a geyser of untranslatable thoughts. But it starts with a Ratpack B-side called *If You Can't Translate a River, How You Gonna Translate the Sea?* and from there things get "worse" which is to say " 'worse' " and the protagonist is a man who forgets all of his body parts so he has labels attached to all of his body parts and labels attached to the labels to remind him what labels are and why he needs them and a tertiary set of labels with caveats. Do the children run from him as he rustles by or point and laugh? Let's be honest. Nobody points and laughs. If I saw someone pointing and laughing I'd point and laugh at them. I remember at the age of 6 I was trying to write the word *treasure* and I asked my teacher how do you spell *zh*? She said *It's entirely dependent on context* and I said *What's context?* You know when you accidentally hug someone too hard and there's a moment where they struggle or say *oof.* What are you trying to do? On my shelf I have a copy of a journal from the 80s called *Poetic Comment* only it's just poems – and they're not great – no comment whatsoever, go figure. Go tell it on the mountain. If I tried to italicize the way I feel about you the letters would lean *so far* to the right they'd be invisible.

ABOUT THE AUTHOR:

Luke Kennard is a poet and novelist. His books have been shortlisted for the Forward Prize, the Desmond Elliott Prize and the International Dylan Thomas Prize. He lectures in the School of English at the University of Birmingham.

BY THE SAME AUTHOR:

Poetry:

The Solex Brothers (2005)
The Harbour Beyond the Movie (2007)
The Migraine Hotel (2009)
Planet-Shaped Horse (2011)
The Necropolis Boat (2012
A Lost Expression (2014)
Cain (2016)

Fiction:

Holophin (2012)
The Transition (2017)

ACKNOWLEDGEMENTS:

Some of these poems have appeared in other forms. Thank you to the editors. I am also grateful to Susannah Dickey and Kadie Newman for reading, insight and advice, and to Stuart Bartholomew at Verve Poetry Press for patience and editorial prowess.